Heart Prints

a dance of heartache and healing

Georgette Ann

Georgette Ann
Cajun Blues Ink, LLC
Louisiana, USA
www.georgetteannwriter.com

ISBN-13: 978-0-578-55248-4

DEDICATION

For my grandparents, Doc and Anna, who were beautiful people inside and out. They were my stability—and in truth, my salvation. I'm not sure where I'd be if they hadn't been so present and loving in my upbringing. A huge part of me died with them, and I still grieve for all the moments we've missed since then. I can only hope they had some sense of how much they impacted my life for the better. Their influence was monumental. I love and miss them so.

CONTENTS

INTRODUCTION

It's not so much that I found words, as they found me. I learned as a child not to draw attention to myself. Everything was easier that way, but it also meant that I became a silent observer of my life, sometimes of life in general. And though I rarely spilled my words, I could taste them like sparks dancing on my tongue. I'd lose myself in books, reveling in the words of others while too afraid to speak my own. The thing about words is that you can't undo them, and that's utterly terrifying. But there's freedom in the release—in the fact that you can breathe life into your thoughts with ink. And whether others love your words or hate them, they are your own to lay bare. It is a cleansing of sorts.

I write to heal.

Georgette Ann

Heart prints—

those snapshots
in time which
cling to us and
forever change

the way we see,
the way we feel,
the way we love.

Georgette Ann

PART I

It is a sobering truth to recognize
you are broken in irreparable ways,
despite all the years and attempts
and methods to mend those
fractured pieces. Knowing that
even though you try to be better
every waking moment, somehow
a darkness lingers. So, you function
within the world's constraints and
hide behind a distant smile and
pen secret words, all in the hope
of saving what's left of you from
utter self-destruction.

Georgette Ann

Losing my voice felt like
slowly suffocating, one
choked word at a time—
until I simply went mute
just to continue breathing.

I vacillated,
even as I sensed
it going south

teetering between
one last try and driving
the nail in the coffin

hanging on to the
thinnest thread
invisible of hope
and promise

though the ending
was written well
before the beginning

and you knew,
but you dangled
it just the same.

Piles of
tattered
photographs,
stained
letters,
and stale
memories
are all that
remain of a
collection of
moments I
once believed
to be love.

Your biggest mistake
was equating my silence
with complacency—

my biggest mistake
was believing my silence
mattered to you.

Slowly, I merge
back into a life
where normal
is abnormal—
a life that is
permanently
skewed by the
absence of you.

It's late, again
I should sleep,
but my demons are
devious insomniacs
with a penchant for
the witching hour
who remind me of
every indiscretion,
of a litany of flaws
real and imagined,
of all the reasons
I'll never be enough
for you, or me, or us—
and I cower at the
thought of exposing
my naked soul to you,
because you just might
see right through me.

In the stillness
of first morning
before the sun
makes her debut

when the veil
of sleep has
barely lifted
from my eyes

among remnants
of lucid dreams,
paled memories—
there I find you.

Words hang
in the air
between us
and letting
them fall
is akin to
standing in
an ocean of
vulnerability
and hoping to
survive the
coming storm.

Beyond butterflies
and wildflower fields
where winds carry puffs
of dandelion wishes

over the rainbow
past the beaten path
where sunbeams wither
among the shadows

under the silent
blackness of night
where secrets go
to live and die

I wait for you—
I wait for you still.

Georgette Ann

I wonder—

if you had
to search
for me
beyond
the blues
of my eyes,

would you
ever be able
to find me?

On nights like
these when the
sun sinks beneath
cotton candy skies—

I feel whispers of
you on balmy breezes
and imagine the words
hiding in your sighs.

I lied when
I told you I
didn't need you
to define us;
in truth, it was
all I needed—
and more.

I'm not sure if
you couldn't
or wouldn't,
only that
you didn't.

And that was
the unraveling
of one heart and
the undoing of two.

And I suddenly
realized distance
often has little to
do with geography.

Deep in the night
I wait, I wait—
for the echoes
of your memory
and the salt from
my eyelashes to
finally release me
into oblivion—
so I might forget
for just a while
that you are not
coming back.

I'm not sure what
bothers me more—

the fact that there is
so much left unsaid
between us, or the
fact that saying it
wouldn't make any
difference at all.

Once I was an oasis
the calm within a storm
like the eye of a hurricane
an escape sans tethers,
until I understood
the whole of it—
to be merely a
temporary sojourn,
never a permanent
destination was
not nearly enough;
thus, I receded
into myself becoming
only a mirage.

I can't help
but wonder—

where do the
flutters of
your heart lie,

if not here
with me?

All you
see is
all I am

it's either
enough
or it isn't

there is
no going
back now

it is what
it is—
or isn't

do what you
must with
what is left.

How I longed
to be her—

the one for whom
your pen bled,
your heart pined

the one who
filled your
every thought

even then, as I
filled your bed.

The heart never
knows quite how
to bury a love
that in the
beginning
was too much,
but in the end
was not enough.

Do not believe
for a moment
that you could
ever break me—

for I've lived
most of my life
on the wrong
side of love,

'neath a shadow
of hopelessness,
survived it all, and

you—well, I will
survive you, too.

The truth is
I am so
much more

and less—

than you ever
saw in me.

Isn't it funny how
memories lurk at
the bottom of
a wine glass and
in 3 a.m. shadows—

when all you can do
is sit and wonder
if he still thinks
of you softly
sometimes, too?

My corner of
the universe
hasn't quite
been the same
since you've
come and gone.

You haunt me
in ways I never
imagined—

your residue
lingering like
fine powder

in all the nooks
and crannies of
an unfinished love.

I couldn't tell
you these things

because you weren't
ready to hear them,

so I let the words
fall onto paper like

lost souls on the
quest for some

deeper meaning I
didn't find in us.

You walk
through
my words,
oblivious
to their
weight, to
my heart—

and this is
precisely why
neither still
belongs to you.

I think
I must be
destined
to be but
a memory
or a ghost—

perhaps,
a little
of both.

You can't emerge
from the shadows
after all this time
telling me you've
only just realized how
much you miss me,
igniting internal fires
as though you mean it—

not after all this time,
not after I've already
laid my heart upon
your altar in vain.

I don't know if
love ever truly dies—
I think maybe it
gradually fades into
unfulfilled promises,
unshared memories,
and unspoken words
that we cling to until
our hearts are strong
enough to let go.

Sometimes
we are not
destinations
but rather
temporary
bridges for
one another—

A number of
finite steps
closing the
gaps between
the marks life
makes upon our
bruised hearts.

Georgette Ann

I think we leave
pieces of ourselves
behind in others—

I'm hoping mine
are among the ones
you'll decide are
worth keeping.

I have thought of you and what
might have been in another time
and place. Perhaps some things are
meant to exist in beautiful bubbles
that touch us in the right moment
and inevitably float on. Life certainly
has a way of giving our hearts
impossible glimpses and leaving
indelible marks in its wake—but
never without reason. There is
always a reason.

Georgette Ann

PART II

You don't realize that you've never
been loved the right way until you
are. What I mean is that you find
yourself being loved by someone who
accepts you in your entirety without
conditions or judgments; that person
champions all that you hold close
and believes in not only what you've
done but what you have yet to do.
And suddenly, you understand how
love is supposed to look and feel.
And then there's no turning back.

Georgette Ann

I built a life of absolutes
upon a foundation of nevers,
forevers, and always;
But it was all structure
and no substance—
a black and white existence
which left little room for
the sometimes, maybes,
and what ifs.
It did not allow for
risk, spontaneity,
or happenstance.
And I realized
I required something more;
I desired something deeper.
I needed all the colors;
I wanted to feel alive.
So I did.

I know it is
a fallible heart
which beats within
this hollow shell of mine.

Still I follow
it with blind hope
and broken dreams
like a lamb into slaughter.

Yellow,
there must
always be yellow—

ribbons and sunlight,
roses and candlelight,
ruffles and moonlight;

She bathes herself
in yellow to chase
away her blue.

I've lost my way,
been abandoned and
discarded, infinitely
misunderstood—

picked up the pieces
of a broken life
and a broken heart
more times than I
care to remember—

yet I'm still here,
ticking boxes off
my list of all the
things I've outlived.

Sunday morning
wakes me slowly
with kisses of
hope and silent
sunbeams casting
shadows over time,

making me believe
maybe I'm not as
broken as I feel.

It is said endings
are beginnings, but
maybe it's just what
we tell ourselves—

a sort of permission
we grant ourselves
to move on, move
forward, just move;

a bit of persuasion
for our hearts to take
a chance, a risk, a leap—

in hope of a soft landing
in the midst of complete
unequivocal uncertainty.

What noble teachers,
age and experience—
coaxing us to let go
while it's still good,

letting us preserve
perfect pockets of
life—however brief,

so they remain pure
and untarnished by
the sting of regret.

Georgette Ann

At last she emerged—
a burgeoning storm,

a kaleidoscope
of desires,

a cacophony
of emotions,

and all kinds
of beautiful.

What am I,
but a mere

collection
of words

waiting to
be whispered

upon a heart
yet unknown?

Some loves barrel
in like a hurricane
demanding to be felt
with equal force—

but by their nature,
die quickly, leaving
chaos in their wake.

Other loves tiptoe in
like the newborn sun
beckoning us with a
slow, rising warmth—

and carrying all the
promise of tomorrow in
soft, honeyed kisses.

What becomes
of a girl
whose heart
has leapt
into a
full-fledged
free fall
of enigmatic
exhilaration?

She discovers
she has wings.

I eluded love,
fearing the risk
wouldn't be worth
the fall; yet you
never wavered—

I think you knew
all along that
my heart would
find its way
home to yours.

Beneath pale
moonbeams
I found what
I thought
to be lost,
lingering
between your
words and
your touch—

Come love,
and watch
me blossom.

Sometimes
we lose
ourselves
in love—

other times
we find
ourselves.

The further
I fall,

the more
I believe

I was made
to love you.

I do not see
myself the way
you see me—

in my entirety,
not as a collection
of frayed edges
and jagged pieces;

and when your eyes
rest on slivers of
light peeking from
cracks in my armor,

I cannot imagine how
you find beauty where
I can only see scars.

I cannot explain
beauty, but I know
it when I see it—

as in the flawless
way my name falls
from your lips.

Georgette Ann

One by one
you discover my
gathered layers—

delicately
exposing bits
of my brokenness;

I wait for you
to find too much
or maybe not enough,

and I'm always a
little taken aback
when I wake to see
you're still here.

Even before
our eyes have
found the light—

I wake to
the softness
of your lips
finding mine.

Georgette Ann

How often do you catch
a glimpse of your eyes
in a mirror or bring a
finger to your lips or
fall asleep with your
hand upon your heart—

without ever realizing
these are all the places
where I relearned the
magic of being a woman?

Undress my soul
as my inhibitions
fall to the floor
at the mercy of
your tender hands
tracing every scar.

Somewhere
here amongst
stardust and
moonbeams,

between two
splintered
hearts and
jagged pasts,

I found hope
in full bloom
and love in
whispers of us.

It is a curious
notion for a girl
who was broken
at the hands
of one man
to believe she
could be healed
at the hands
of another—

yet here you are
loving me
back together,
as though it is
the most natural
thing in the world.

Love me
like there's
no tomorrow—

so even for
a moment,

I might feel
a lifetime
between us.

To say I would
be nothing
without you
would be a lie—

I will always
be something,
but I would not
be this me—

the one who
scales walls
instead of
builds them.

When there are
no more words—

there is only
the merging
of the colors
of our souls.

All my life,
I only knew
growth borne
from pain—

the quiet strength
of survival that
forces you to rise
and continue on;

I didn't know it
was possible to
grow through love,
to bloom in the
arms that hold you.

Georgette Ann

Sometimes
the world
grows
too much
within me,
and I need
only to melt
into the
hollows of
your grooves
to find
the edges
of my soul
once more.

I remember it
distinctly—

the moment
your soul
reached out

and touched
mine—as if
to say, hey

I remember you.

If only I
had known
you would
be waiting
at the end
of all my
heartache,

I would have
gotten here
sooner.

I've no idea
how it is
that you know
when I need
sheltering, but
surrendering
to your arms
always feels
like coming home.

There are
these moments
where time
blinks, and
I can see
myself through
your eyes—

and for the
first time in
forever, I know
this is how I
was meant to
be loved.

Heart Prints

It's so hard for
me to lay down
my burdens, to
surrender them.
I've carried them
alone for so long,
I don't know how to
measure my worth
without them—
yet here you are
admiring my strength
even as you quietly
pick up the pieces I
can no longer hold,
and I love you for it.

75

And what
better
evidence
of love
is there
than the
sheltering
of one soul
by another?

When love truly heals, it brings
peace to a broken soul. The holes
begin to fill in trickles and spurts,
and then eventually in waves. It is
the tender cleansing that quells the
incessant longing. The restlessness
evaporates subtly, leaving a perfect
stillness. And there is only the silent
contentment of a heart that can
breathe freely at last. Your love did
this—it will always be you.

Georgette Ann

PART III

Ours is a quiet love borne of second
chances and newfound hope. It
lives in fresh blooms amid moonlight
kisses. It is your hands in the small
of my back, my lips in the crook of
your neck. It beckons us like the
ocean to unexplored depths and
uncharted courses. It is unhurried
mornings painted in sunbeams,
tangled in limbs. This love is a
godsend for two hearts gently
navigating the vulnerability of
surrender. It is our truth.

Georgette Ann

You'll know
me when
you see me—

I'll be
the one
with
flowers
in her hair
and love
on her lips.

I believe the
most potent
love is the one
that takes you
by surprise,
the one that
finds you when
you expect it
least—like an
ambush of the
heart that you
could never
defend yourself
against, even if
you wanted to.

Once in a lifetime
perhaps, a girl
meets that someone

whose absence is
as palpable to her
soul as his presence,

and her heart knows
it to be love.

I dreamt of you again
last night and woke
to find echoes of
your whispers strewn
about my pillow
like warm kisses
waiting to be felt.

I float—

tethered by
heart strings

my world tipped
faintly off axis

ever since I
tasted forever

on your lips.

You gaze at me
every morning
and every evening
with adoring eyes—

as though you
cannot see
the scars which
stitch my soul
together;

And I have never
been so thankful
for the feigned
blindness of love.

I can think
of nothing
more poetic
than the
tender dance
between our
silhouettes
deep into
the night.

The most incredible
feeling is waking
to the pulse of your
heartbeat against
my own and knowing
it beats for me.

Do you know what
it is to love
without restraint?

It is both
Heaven
and hell—

the adventure
of a lifetime,
the measure of
heartbeats and
heartbreaks, the
breathing of one
soul into another.

Georgette Ann

You read me
and I lie exposed,
translucent even—
under the weight
of your soul.

In the
instant
my heart
knew you
to be love,
it was the
beginning of
everything
I know to
be true.

Georgette Ann

I'm not sure
what it means,
the way I begin
and end my day
exactly the
same everyday—

bathed in
moonlight and
nestled in
the crook
of your neck,

but I think
just maybe
it's magic.

Here
I am,
completely
unbound to
anything—
except you.

My words
are not lost;
they are
suspended
in the breaths
between us—

caught up in
all these
bits of love
that have
taken hold of
my heart.

You linger
here above
my heart,
for you are
home—

And I
know this;
this love
is poetry.

I like to watch
you sleep, to feel
the faint whisper
of your breath
against the curve
of my shoulder,
the strength of
your silhouette
paired with mine
after you've taken
me and brought
me here, to this
incredible place
called love.

Heart Prints

Sunday flows
like molasses,
sweet and
oh so smooth

like a southern drawl
draped in August,
sauntering
through my veins
soothing me,
moving me—

Sunday is everything
I love about us
wrapped up in these
moments and heartbeats—
your soul woven into mine.

If I
know
nothing
else,

I know
you are
my saving
grace.

I love you
in ways
even I don't
comprehend—
complete
and true,

as though
it's always
been here
waiting to
be unearthed,

like the first
glow of morn
on dewdrop
kissed petals.

You and those
fathomless
ocean eyes
beckon me

to plunge to
your depths
while I gasp
for air—

tempting me
to drown in
you, over and
over again.

The disquiet
of my heart
is tamed only
by the taste
of your lips.

For a girl
who has never
felt at home
anywhere ever,

I am blissful
and content
just here—

in this love,
in this life,
as I've never
been before.

On the
ethereal
dawn of
Spring

I find
my soul
undeniably
tangled
with yours,

blooming
in the garden
of our
ever after.

One of my
favorite
places
to be is
in your
smile.

On those
mornings
when you
rise while
I drift in
slumber,

it is the
whispered
kisses you
leave upon
my shoulders
that linger
in my sweet
dreams of you.

I need
little
else but
this—

your hand
and
your heart
over mine.

From the very
first time,
you've always
taken me with
an honest heart;

your every touch
uncovering my
deepest truth—
I don't need
to be rescued,
only loved;

And that is how
you came to be
my savior.

Do you know
that in loving me
faithfully and oh,
so fiercely—
you've taught me
not only how to love,
but how to let myself
be loved in return?
And thus, my love
unequivocally,
undeniably—
belongs to you.

With each
soft brush
of your lips,
every gentle
stroke of
your hand,
each tender
sway of
your body
against mine—

you paint a
masterpiece
of this love.

I searched
my entire
life for the
feeling of
being in
your arms.

These moments
in which you
suspend time
and steal
my breath—

and I submit
blissfully
under your
spell, again
and again.

There's no need
to wonder where
we go from here,

this place where
our hearts dance
on ordinary days
and electric nights,
in the flourishing
of profound love—

there is no where
to go; for, we are
already here.

And if this
were the end,
the moment
breath ceased
to ignite life
into my soul—

I would lie at
peace, knowing
at last I loved
and was loved
with a heart
that was both
raw and pure.

I love you—

nothing more,
nothing less;

And yet—

it is
everything.

I wake in the dead of night to the
brush of your breath against my skin.
Like a silent plume, it reminds me
with every gentle stroke that you are
here—even when you are not. And I
turn into you, so that our breath
mingles and I might feel all that you
are against all that I am not.

Georgette Ann

There
is no
alluring
mystery
here—

only the
penning of
a girl's soul
through a
woman's hand.

Georgette Ann

ACKNOWLEDGEMENTS

To my husband, my greatest muse and biggest champion. Without you, none of this would be possible. Thank you for believing in me. Words cannot express how happy you've made me. Even a lifetime is not long enough to show you how much I truly love you, but I will never stop trying.

To my children, who make me believe that I am badass even though I'm mostly not. Thank you for being my unwavering cheerleaders. You are my heart. I love you with everything I am.

To my mom, who sparked my creativity by buying a typewriter for me in 1979. Thank you for always encouraging me to follow my dream. I love you.

To my real life soul sisters, a group of incredibly strong and talented women who continually inspire me to be a better woman, mother, and friend. Thank you for always having my back without question. You really are badass, and I love you all.

To my internet soul sisters, a group of phenomenal women who build others up and support them. In taking me under your wings, you helped me find my own. Thank you for your constant examples of courage, strength, and love. Love and hugs.

Georgette Ann

AUTHOR'S NOTE

I've been writing since I can remember. My mom gave me a two-tone blue Sears manual typewriter for my eighth birthday, and I wore that little blueberry out. Then she gave me a Sears Graduate One electric model when I graduated high school. And I wore that one out, too. I have journals and manuscripts tucked away that other eyes have never seen—dozens of stories and vignettes. I only started writing poetry 5 years ago at age 43. It seemed to be the right form of expression at the time. And some wild thing in me made me share it publicly, despite my fear. I suppose I just couldn't contain my words any longer. And that is how I came to know all of you beautiful people. So, thank you for reading the stains my heart leaves upon these pages and for being a part of my journey.

Georgette Ann

CONNECT ON SOCIAL MEDIA

Web:
www.georgetteannwriter.com

Facebook:
facebook.com/georgetteann.writer

Instagram:
@georgetteann.writer

Tumblr:
https://georgetteann-writer.tumblr.com

Twitter:
@cajunbluesink

Pinterest:
https://www.pinterest.com/cajunbluesink/

Georgette Ann

CPSIA information can be obtained
at www.ICGtesting.com
Printed in the USA
LVHW041034151019
634129LV00023B/3996/P